*The Country of Perhaps*

CHRIS McCULLY was born in Yorkshire in 1958. He is Senior Lecturer in English at the University of Manchester. His previous collections of poetry include *Time Signatures* (1993) and *Not Only I* (1996), and he edited *The Poet's Voice and Craft* (1994).

Also by Chris McCully from Carcanet

*Time Signatures*
*Not Only I*

*The Poet's Voice and Craft* [Editor]

# CHRIS McCULLY

## *The Country of Perhaps*

**CARCANET**

First published in 2002 by
Carcanet Press Limited
4th Floor, Conavon Court
12-16 Blackfriars Street
Manchester M3 5BQ

A CIP catalogue record for this book
is available from the British Library
ISBN 1 85754 550 8

The publisher acknowledges financial assistance
from the Arts Council of England

Set in 10pt Bembo by Bryan Williamson, Frome
Printed and bound in England by SRP Ltd, Exeter

# Contents

For Gavin Smith

## Acknowledgements

Several people read these poems in draft, and suggested changes. I'm particularly grateful to Dana Gioia, Howard Osborn, Janet McCully, Gavin Smith, Anne Stevenson, and Gareth Twose for pointing out miscalculations and mistakes.

Many of the poems in Part One appeared in *PN Review*, and I'm grateful to the editor for permission to reprint here. 'Fishermen on Santa Monica Pier' was a runner up in the 1998 *Stand International Poetry Competition*, and was published in *Stand*. Fragments from *Mass* appeared in *Time Signatures* (Carcanet, 1993) and *Not Only I* (Carcanet, 1996), and I am once again grateful to Michael Schmidt for permission to reprint these fragments in their new, and proper, context. The epigraph to 'Steel and Glass' is from W.H. Auden, 'A Knight of Doleful Countenance', in *Forewords and Afterwords* (Faber, 1973).

CHRIS McCULLY
*Amsterdam, 2000*

# PART ONE

## The Country of Perhaps

_____

## An Ashtray for San Francisco

The errant boys are falling into light
from memories of speed and Viet Nam.
Some opened restaurants. Some retain the right
to remain silent in their book of names
and shake all morning. 'What a fuck I am
to end up bumming dimes on Folsom Street.'
Some bought their Harleys just to hit the heat
across the Golden Gate
as every gimcrack analyst declaims
'Where did the bad experiences start?'
A drugstore, midnight, and a broken heart.

Don't Walk. Don't spit don't ride don't smoke don't cough.
Remember how to grease. And park in line.
On 8th Street it's $5 to jack off
and mumblers to themselves replay the hurt
whose accusations, daddy, made them shine
on vodka and a cup of coins. In bookstores
full of laptops professorial bores
chew nonsense in loose jaws
and windy graduates almost making out
are theorists of the uselessness of art:
cold coffee, midnight, and a broken heart.

You flew in from Vancouver, and were zoned,
wild-eyed in Haight, the body-stocking ripped.
'Marijuana. Over One Billion Stoned'
and looking for another dry embrace
to fend the fear that loneliness equipped
and wandered with in city streets all day.
'That bitching Rhonda. Thinks her shit is grace.'
Your $15 was too much to pay
to watch his come deface your resumé.
'He got his manners straight from AutoMart',
a rat-faced midnight and a broken heart.

'A silly thing I have to figure out . . .'
His Jaeger G-string . . . And she's doing dope,
some tenement on 9th Street:
messed up the rhythms as the childhood hope
begins to bleed away
however far. 'And I can't hear her shout . . .'
Meanwhile the errant boys are falling, falling
through all the hurt that was the last good lay,
and someone has forgotten that they're calling
a double-take – from LAX to JFK –
whose tears are on the make, but scald. And smart
the midnight, smart
the drugstore, smart
the crooked heart.

*San Francisco and Sonoma County, 1999*

# Icarus

He was mad with it:
the intricacies of construction,
the wax that sealed each joint
to a workable point,
the local clarities of angles,
feathers, whatever could explain
the assemblage and harness it
to the dynamics of the sky.

He was mad with it,
and as the air glazed
without effort under the beating wings,
as the olive groves and the blue zoo
of the sea receded merely
to hillsides and ocean,
a disarticulated view,
he had succeeded.

He was mad with it,
the whole beautiful engineering.
But turning westwards, higher,
becoming pressure, becoming weight,
he had forgotten the sun.
And strange that when there was
that endless sense of falling,
he was glad of it.

# Cuckoo

Ill-omened bird, bridling and dowdy, you
seemed instinct in the six-times-urgent eggs
of everyone into whose nest you flew.

And now you twat about on rotten legs
pretending to be thrush, a broken heart,
the voice of summer every bad poet begs.

You sit on fenceposts with your voice apart,
two syllables of murder in the rain.
No pain for birds like you. You killed for art.

## Lipstick

Carefully, carefully
you made yourself up,
watching each line
of eyebrow, of top lip:

another performance
I'd watch for love,
seeing the construction
that skin would give.

Perfect, perfect,
you turned away satisfied,
but the city was burning,
the gaze has decayed

since it found in the mirror
behind the stare
the something that was missing,
the nothing there.

# Demeter

I'm the summer's pride, the heart of the corn,
the swallow's sickle, the circle
of the not yet died
and of the unborn.

I'm summer's lease, the cash in the till,
the wet footprint in the shower,
the hour and then another hour
of the ignorable ill.

I'm summer's heart, the beat
of the drum in the barley straw,
the dressed-up festival, the masks, the bore,
the not worth living for.

I'm harvest, the olive trees,
crushed oil and seized grape,
the gift of life.
I promised only imperfection,
was almost everyone's wife.

# Death Valley

'We heard of the bank vaults, the breakable acres,
the impossible strikes and charms,'
said the mouths as they sucked at the future.
But the sand–devils hissed back 'Harms.'

'Where are the fabulous gravels, the silvers,
the ores to braze into gold?'
cried the voices in the salt of the desert.
And the mountains echoed 'Old.'

'Where are wild horses, and endless whiskey,
and burros with panniers to fill?'
asked need through its stained bandannas.
And the burst stone whispered 'Ill.'

'Here's the dynamite. Here's the blue vein.
Here are the tracks of my friends,'
said the hand in his heyday to the water-jar
and the canyon's warning, 'Ends.'

'I've made the deposit, I've riddled the sunlight,
I've starved in the whore's deck of worth.
I've mined a hard million – but where am I going?'
And the dry river-bed coughed, 'Earth.'

'Why is there blood on the edge of the shovel?
Why am I so alone?'
asked the end of the journey to the red rich rock.
And the pick-axe answered 'Own.'

'Is there anything left? Is anyone there?
Rare, rare as desert snow,
does the future come softly to save me and solve me?'
And the silence of Leadfield spoke. 'No.'

*Death Valley, California, 1996*

17

## Fishermen on Santa Monica Pier

Real life's defeated them across the world.
Wherever it may be –
from Santa Monica to the Red Sea –
they've always been old, always seen the waves
hush around the pier's end hurt as hope,
evolved a deepening shadow on the skin
and watched the sun go down, nothing to show
but the slow hours connected to a weight
where age is waiting, become
imaginary as the sun,
though it comes too late to riddle back,
to solve their going home again alone
with a mind full of photographs and bone;
ling, bass and huss; cut bait;
and that specific of the moon,
the lost ability to concentrate.

They spin their hands through shoals of pull and touch
to find simplicity, to wish the flood
come live, as if the act could prove
the past was tractable, made to behave
into a trick of eye and light, and now
the riding of a float hard by a stave . . .
They last real life, happen on all their ghosts
across the world whose country is Perhaps
and happiness, that lies much otherwise
than handbooks of the self assume,
and can't be gained by going or by maps.
But by connectedness and choice
of being where the end of age has happened
and is working out its furies in the deep
amendments of what brought it close,
they stand for silence and its gravities.

*Venice, California, 1996*

18

## *Watching the Cherry*

An astonishing pink
  cherry-tree
collides with me.

Down April it put on
its celebration.
All month it grew
  a little more familiar,
    a little more
       askew.

Now the topmost boasts
of blossom toss
as May winds cross
the quays, the slates, the skies.

I think of you these days
again and again,
watching the cherry emptying
in the small winds, the small rain.

## Bearings

From Bertraghboy all bearings take a line
        on Cashel mountain's mark
to clear Treh Island, Oghly, Croaghmore.
The summit happens as a kind of sign.
        Even in almost dark
it's what a navigator's looking for,

is where the compass can be fixed, and start
        to govern comings-in,
to keep keel sound up to a rope and quay.
A hull of hill has circumstanced the chart
        through seaward discipline:
to take a bearing is a making free.

*Cashel, Connemara, 1996*

## Migrants

I was the point of the poor
field of the famine year,
rash of the tuber's aim.
I was the hunchback bride
and the kelp in the tide.
I've forgotten my name.

I was the face in the stone
whose voice was buried unborn
in the sail's hull.
I was the one who paid
the hunger you made.
I was the hill's skull.

I was the journey to come,
the weight in the empty room,
the navigable star.
I was the language you spoke
when your spirit broke
across America.

*Cashel, Connemara, 1996*

# Steel and Glass

'. . . Narcissus fell in love with his reflection, not out of conceit but out of despair of finding another who will listen and respond' (W.H. Auden)

### I

Chased metals; the steel rose
that is the touch you chose
whose laceration's thorn
is glass – exact, undrawn.

Intent to torch a face
out of the hurt of grace,
you find yourself again
amending the old pain.

Impossible to ignore
skin was like this before
age riddled back its days
to find a stranger's gaze.

### II

No longer
fascinated by the stranger
he tries to turn his eyes
from their own glaze.

He can't.
His looking won't relent,
but has no chance to mate
his counterfeit.

To forget
the structures of regret,
to find the past annulled
but still enthralled:

the release,
knowing the time must choose
not the ones never there
but the one here.

## Always

I don't believe your always
is what always must always mean.
Everything always changes
and leaves always unclean.

An ex is sex in flux,
good looks don't always last.
You've read too many books
about always in the past.

Goodbye is always better.
It always won't trust you.
It hated your last letter –
but then, I always do.

What always weighs the same
is the weight of ex-farewell.
Erasure of a name
is always. Kiss. Don't tell.

## Conversation Piece

You don't mention it, of course –
the child's death, the divorce,

the social worker's terse report;
her carefully controlled
breakdown in court.

You don't mention it, and pour
another shot of whatever it is.
It no longer has ice in the fizz, I notice.
It's what you're still living for.

'I got over all that,' you say, slurred
after the third.
What hurts is how she left you when
it seemed you'd patched it up. Again

you're going rotten.
You hoped you'd forgotten.

'Have to move on,
yes.' But the shock
is where you go, and how when once you've gone
you never come back.

## Smoke Rings in October

Another pack of Amber Leaf,
As frail as mist, as cheap as grief.
She looks past traffic, looks past rain:
Tomorrow isn't happening.
What's happening is the kind of thing
He likes, laughed at, before the pain.

Who bought the flowers? Nicely cut.
Sprays of some lily. Too much white.
Somewhere the noise of news goes pale.
Why did he have to laugh at all?
She shakes the box that's turned half-full
And taps it, nicotine and nail.

## Whoever

Whoever you force you fill
with moments falling to a kind of grace,
then make them ill
down the long wastes of the body's need
all night, but keep the kindness on the face
despite the sickness and the seed.

Rocked by morning, you
get up to wash the fracture and the stain,
to watch the blue
amendments defacing the taut skin.
Again you wish it otherwise. Again
whoever could be anyone.

## At Lindisfarne Priory

In the beginning
there were no *Safe Crossing Times*:
remote the place,
endowed with stone and hope,
and tide ceaseless
as the activity of grace.

Succeeding names defined
access of a kind:
Aidan, Cuthbert, Chad –
whose words charmed
animals from the ocean,
weapons from woundings,
to the miraculous wood.

They understood
how prayer has to exist
as the voice of causeways and edges
and lives in windows where there's nothing
but coloured fragments of a day,
a hill growing out of a beach,
and the blue impossible sky
that's always but not quite
out of reach.

## A pen is

Unwise; undone. Everyone said
too rash, and prophesied the mad

amendments of a short affair
gone wrong. Here, there and everywhere

dinners by gossiping decreed
a razor's edge; that heads would bleed.

Perhaps the voices of Alas
were right; but how much righter was

the voice that candidly advised
a pen is always compromised –

'Never go out with poets. They
just want to write the elegy.'

## Casterbridge

I know you well enough, Michael Henchard –
how you sold your wife
into the country of Perhaps;
how drink's bitters stirred your life
into the long years of redemption;
how it was always
the waiting and the failure of waiting;
how you were unredeemed.

I know you well enough to know
your darling must have seemed
the envy of every knowledge,
a strangeness jealous of all strangers.
Only what began to grow
at the mind's root was the weight
of the traffic of bought grain,
and when you lifted the trap-stone
whose heaviness was love,
expecting the love
to come pouring into space and place,
then trouble starved the darling
and failure of your voice.
I know you well enough, Michael Henchard –
you and your choice.

## Song at Midnight

just why
    the blackbird sings at midnight I
        don't know

lamps glow
    along the docks
        perhaps it's that

some quality of light
    too early to be true
        comes clear as dawn

and still
    the blackbird frets
        as if it's ill

blood in its throat
    I use each note
        to think of debts

mistakes
    words waste and aches
        the days gone wrong

but for the song
    I wouldn't work so late
        or wait

## Manners

He left the girl, the girl left him –
the girl with the manners called heartbreak
whose excuses wore thin.

She left the man, the man left her –
the man with the manners called midnight
and the Polar star.

Ruin runs outwards from its oldest source.
Tomorrow will come but be different,
beloved. Of course

they left each other, the ruin went on
into the manners that were left in the future
which hoped there were none.

## Moving On

For all the illusions of new starts, keep going,
        and think who'll be
unlucky enough to get the stuff you've thrown.
Not even charity? No way of knowing
the dog-chewed bits of bloodline, sympathy,
ill-chosen words and frames will find a home.

Your mother's double bed stands in the garden.
        Incipient rain.
In the attic where you learnt to work and swear
the glue on once-used tools has come to harden
on joints set forty years ago; on pain.
The dust defines itself. It doesn't care.

## Serbia
### for Marija Radakovic

The bar keeper
in this taverna
is a student doctor
from Serbia.

Here for the summer,
her future
was learned from a
drunk teacher,

her English from a
friend's grammar.
'*Kalispera*, doctor.'
'Good evening, writer.'

Her egg-shell face
is going to feature
blood, bone and suture.
And she'll give them grace.

*Crete, 1997*

## The Birth

The Bureau of Reproductive Technology
engendered him as 19/D.3.
There were no complications. No one cried.
He had replaced a need conveniently.
We were satisfied.

## Presents

You pulled the new dress from its dollars
and thought about Christmas Day.
You tried on the dress for the mirror
that couldn't run away.
And what did the mirror reply, my dear?
That you were the fairest, the perfect, the brave?
A talented body that knew how to behave?
      O no, my dear, my love. That was sex,
      but what mirrors say is meant as a hex,
      and the mirror's reply
          was I.

You took the new shoes from the shoe-box,
and thought that they'd suit your career.
You arranged your hair in the toe-caps
as the leather started to leer.
Did the one that looked back leer or smile, my love?
Did it want a clear skin and an angled jaw?
Did it wonder what that briefest of frowns was for?
      O no, my fox, my coney, my dear.
      The gaze you found had already found fear,
      and what fear must deny
          is I.

You unwrapped the ring from its tissues,
and thought about value and price.
You slipped it on your third finger
then took it off, twice.
And what was the ruby's reflection, my angel?

It had no chance to answer. It had seen your face
taut with contempt, marked by disgrace.
      And yes, my dear. What the mirror had bred
      was beauty, but what you'd seen instead
      was what lies in the eye
          of I.

## From the Country of Perhaps

It's always there, the country of Perhaps,
where it's an agreeable time to be betrayed
into the arms of a middle-aged cocktail waitress
and the warmth of a plausible high-rise bar
where the music is satisfyingly loud
and of no particular vintage
and no one knows or cares who you are –
or at least so you'd like to think
as you sip something quixotic
that's normally far too expensive to drink.

And of course it's a place where a public style
can usually be found for the private shames
of a face made ugly by repeating its sins
or not being able to finish the crossword.
There, too, the hesitant figures
who reel into the night and trip over hydrants
really can still play the movements of
complex sonatas and will see in the mirror
come morning a shape and gesture they can love.

You think it's not to be visited? Too far away?
No, no, and nearer than you imagine.
Just look at your watch-face for a moment –
the appointments, disappointments, the alarms,
and the mystery of six different
but simultaneous time-zones where your schedule
will be kept and meant maybe once only but then
ramify and be unexpected forever.
No wonder you need your shades to confront
how multiple your ends; and the others . . .

At least these inhabitants have things in common:
all have been tempted to flee and driven
at some cost down the eight-lane highways of guilt
where one-night hotels beckon them in
with neon arabesques and the offer
of complimentary *hors d'oeuvres*.
Their credit, like yours, is into the red.
They also hope for the ocean and look wistful
when easy deaths turn ugly, and photographs
of the dog-eared innocent are displayed with pride.

And all have made the valiant effort
at least for a moment to pursue
the moral imperatives of a changed life:
you can see how much it has taken,
how hard it is merely for them to be there,
confused by their passions, not knowing
how to use the cutlery or what to wear
or about tomorrow or whether to send,
postmarked from the country of Perhaps,
the letter that means less than they intend.

*Los Angeles, 1995*

# PART TWO

## Mass

### A poem for voices

---

For Anne Stevenson

'The mass and majesty of this world, all
    That carries weight and always weighs the same . . .'

W.H. Auden, 'The Shield of Achilles'

# Mass

| **Part One** | I: Introit |
| | II: Kyrie |
| | III: Gloria |
| | IV: Sanctus and Credo |
| | V: Stabat Mater |

| **Part Two** | VI: Homily (Judas) |

| **Part Three** | VII: Agnus Dei |
| | VIII: Benedictus |
| | Magnificat |
| | Dona nobis pacem |

## The voices

*Voices #1-3*
*Mary Magdalene (a spinster)*
*Miriam (a middle-aged blind woman)*
*Elisabeth (an old woman)*
*Judas (a sharply-dressed hustler)*
*John (an aged drunk)*

**Note and acknowledgement:** The quotation on p.57 is from John Henry Newman, *Apologia Pro Vita Sua* (Everyman, 1993). Two sections of the present text, from the *Gloria* and the *Stabat Mater*, first appeared in *Time Signatures* (Carcanet, 1993) and *Not Only I* (Carcanet, 1996) respectively. I am also grateful to Sharon Hilles and to the dedicatee of this piece, Anne Stevenson, for their careful and critical readings of draft versions of the present text.

## Part One

### I: INTROIT

*Infelix ego*

**Mary M**:   You know and I know no mind has mass
more than a surgeon's steel can claim –
soft stuff you've seen coiled on a butcher's tray.
But it's not that which came to pass
here: although a mind can give this name
and gravity of tongues, all it can say
would, like pain, have happened anyway.

**Voice #1**:   Something you were. Something had to take place.
Carved out of air and darkness once
a mind began to act, not to weigh,
assumed the lineaments that made a face
melted into its proper part by chance,
made flesh, and you. Whatever you can say
it would, like love, have happened anyway.

**Voice #2**:   If mind's no mass, enactment doesn't weigh,
what weighs? The brutal ceremony of light:
who watches you sees nothing but the dust
disturbed in all the rooms you walk today –
shadows resisting windows; coming night.
You say you don't believe it, but you must:
you took place, you came to pass, were dust in sun,
And mass is just a theory of the sun.

## II: KYRIE

*Puer natus est nobis*

**Voice #3:**    You won't have heard of me. Anywhere in your books
you could ask thirteen different characters the same
and get incomprehension, less a smile. Blank looks

I've lived with. Two millennia, and still no name.
And yet: *Behold, there came wise men from the East*
who carried favour out of time, a kind of fame

or so you're told. It wasn't like that in the least . . .

**Voice #2:**    – without visas or the proper documentation
    – whose papers had traded for a short time in Istanbul
    – whose politics were a stained towel between a girl's legs
    – whose panic ran from the firestorm looking for someone
        to throttle . . .

In this world virgins are raped and there are no miracles.

★

**Voices #1-3:**

| | |
|---|---|
| You won't have heard of me | Always anonymous |
| No part in politics | I kept my nose clean |
| You've got no evidence | Nothing to recognise |

Bethlehem, Bethlehem

| | |
|---|---|
| It was a mystery | Happened so long ago |
| All too much trouble | Too hard to remember it |
| Nothing to do with me | Nothing to place me there |

Bethlehem, Bethlehem

| | |
|---|---|
| There was a register | Feet rushing paving-stones |
| Payment of income tax | Soldiers in passageways |
| Air full of quarrelling | Nights full of argument |

Bethlehem, Bethlehem

*Kyrie eleison*

Why do you want to know?     Keep your face out of it
Can't say for certain now     Strangers were everywhere
All rooms were occupied     Panic paid the tenancy

Bethlehem, Bethlehem

Some had no documents     No proper identity
Sleeping on mattresses     Out with the animals
Hiding as darkness fell     Avoiding the search-parties

Bethlehem, Bethlehem

One day then another     One face and another
What could distinguish them?     Misery looks the same
Anger and misery     Nothing particular

Bethlehem, Bethlehem

*Christe eleison*

You're from the government     I've seen your kind before
No point in asking me     What was one family more?
Perhaps we've heard of him     You've jogged my memory

Bethlehem, Bethlehem

People remarked on it     Thought it odd afterwards
Is this off the record?     One night in December . . .

**Judas:**

*One evening in December witnesses in Bethlehem reported seeing the birth of a new star in the eastern sky. The king's astrologers have since claimed that the alleged sighting was due to climatic aberrancies, but local farmers remain unconvinced. One, who did not wish to be named, said*

**Voices #1-3:**

You won't have heard of me     You've got no evidence
Nothing to do with me     Strangers were everywhere
There was no room for them     Is this off the record?

Bethlehem, Bethlehem

Nothing particular

*Kyrie eleison*

**Judas**:          The sky is dark and there are no resurrections.

                                    ★

**Voices #1-3**:

          But for us there were no resurrections.
          Certainly there was a birth, not what was expected.
          Blood soaked in straw; the smell of dung and breathing;
          another parent saying this was Elijah.
                    Laughable, really.

          These days there are too many prophets
          burnt by the desert, turning into heatwaves.
          Too many troublemakers. Too many warnings
          of weak government. I asked, anyway.
                    Not that it mattered.

          They'd crawled out of the Negev with the others.
          What do I know? Except it felt rather foolish
          standing with nothing to say but disappointment.
          Still, our leaders are notoriously fickle –
                    don't have the breeding.

          There was a row, of course. Something and nothing.
          And no time to ask whoever they were what was meant
          by the fact that for us there are no resurrections.
          We saw what we had gone to see; and went.
                    We'd done our duty.

     *Lord, have mercy*
     *Christ, have mercy*
     *Lord, have mercy*

In the bleak midwinter

*Thine is the kingdom*

44

## III: GLORIA

*Gloria in excelsis Deo*

**Voice #1**:

Who knows best how to write glory,
when glory's never around?
And if all of us went to look for glory,
would glory like to be found?
If we looked in the river, dug up the park,
if we searched each December right into the dark,
there's be no glory, not even one –
the idea of glory's a scam and a con;
and even if there ever was a glory,
glory's gone underground.

**Voice #2**:

Ah yes, well, since you ask about glory . . .
It's never in the same place twice.
One minute it'll be in the Bunsen,
the next in the microscope slice.
It'll be in the entrance, then hang on a peg;
then talk from the back of a donkey's hind leg.
It won't know you're looking, won't even care;
but the thing about glory is, it's always there,
and you'll know that it's somewhere about because
its manners aren't terribly nice.

**Voice #3**:

So if we were to go looking for glory,
you're saying it's a bit of a thug –
an ambush, an outlaw, a bolt from the blue,
an hallucinogenic drug?
But we're right and we're sober; we don't want all that.
We want glory to tread on our new Welcome mat,
to shine from our windows so the neighbours will see,
to string from the lights of our croquet-lawn tree –
in short, we want the sort of glory
you'd engrave on a coffee mug.

45

*Voice #1*:

> But glory's not wanting, won't come at a whistle
> whenever you purse your lips;
> can't be bought, or paid for, signed in a register,
> slipped over fingertips.
> Although it's in time, it's stranger and stronger;
> ticks in the clocks only lasts all the longer;
> doesn't change, isn't ornament, but is there in each cell
> and what each cell comes to in turning out well.
> But you can't ever grasp it, squeeze it, seize it,
> however hard your hand grips . . .

*Voice #2*:

> These are simply abstractions. Where's something definite –
> say, something you'd give to our friends for us?
> Nothing you've said so far writes any cheques for us;
> nothing there makes amends for us.
> Is it like dreaming, there from the start?
> Is it ideas? Or justice? Or art?
> Is it somehow reciting the past to itself
> till the words unwork time in the books on the shelf?
> Or is it like *No* said over and over –
> something that simply defends for us?

*Voice #3*:

> None of the arguments make any sense
> Since glory can't be Yes or No.
> Glory's the nothing that everything was
> when its future began long ago.
> You were included – come to that, so was I:
> neither was conjured from absence and sky
> but was there in the moments that changed what and who
> into history intending us both to be true.
> It's a bit like a photograph, grainy but detailed,
> starting as acid on snow . . .

★

*John*:

The world begins with a black click, and dark
resumes its memory of itself, and lasts
as if nothing had happened in the mark
light briefly made. But there the various pasts –

the fractured children, weddings, hills and trees,
occasions no one noticed in the drink –
are held and muster, living in a frieze
the shutter spooled to keep in every blink.

Instants all wound up. What fills each frame
isn't important; just that it was there,
still is, is necessary for the name
it will be given, will have meant to bear.

Everything was present from the start:
the hand that fired the button is unknown,
but purpose makes its knowledge into art
and slow interpretation, flesh and bone . . .

Development: white paper grows to mountains,
evolves its blistered texture into dares
no one will win, athletics, sisters, fountains
whose laughing boys die smashed in city squares.

Their eyes and situations learned to lie;
the dark-room turns them out routinely real
and following you everywhere like sky
or words or water. They were what you feel –

inheritors of livings crossed with yours
whose purposes come clear but maybe never
until the sun your image lived withdraws
and leaves you ashen, scattered down forever

whose point and all its making's dark again.
Look at the photographs, the mirror: you
loom from nothing like a sweating stain.
And yet that is your miracle come true.

If true these presences, then give to those
you cared for care of you, from first to wife,
the definition of glory: grace that grows
until its endless edges hold a life.

★

*Elisabeth*:
Where did this begin?
Not with the travelling hand,
not with the gravelled paper,
not with a person or a land,
not with this voice behind the chin.

This was accidental, this was thrown
from year to year like history,
from mouth to mouth like dust;
this is the sound of an old mystery –
the noise time passes, like your own:

a dry scrape, leaves on a road,
the ticking of insects in a summer light,
the itch of words as you turn the pages,
the hiss of whisky in a glass at midnight –
provisional silences you're owed.

But where did they begin?
In flesh, the rage of skin on skin,
in alluring places of unease,
in ghosts of marriage-beds, the body's resin,
in beer, or blood, or tin –

too far back now ever to tell:
a word-haunting, love in the dark,
an animal ambition for itself;
a poisoned finger in the park;
an ego-hill; the memory-well.

*Mary M*:

    This was *Yes* in throats torn
           by the edges of hours, minutes as they passed;
           by the shattering of faces in mirrors;
           by the weight of seeing through what fades at last
           into purpose, knowledge; into being born.

★

*Voice #1*:

        Here is the first world. In its first tree
        the breeze breaks into birdsong, early light,
        and leaves riddle with words: BEAUTY and DEATH
        are hung in gold capitals; still wet with night
        SIN and WISDOM lift into shaken stars
        in the first world drawing its native breath.

        The heavens' matter ticked round galaxies.

        Of the possible futures, one was ours
        and necessary, chosen out of pain.
        The human gift for wreckage made its powers
        endure their given lexicon again,
        this time for good. Another tree showed how
        to understand the Word that weighed it now.

# IV: Sanctus and Credo

## Sanctus

*John*:

What matters most is the mind's midnight
whose dream was all the dark I had to go
while others slept too deep in sleep
and with no words to tell I was the Word.

I (who am I) saw what seemed a tree, a trinity
of branches taut with light torn from the air
becoming brighter, brighter still the crossbeam
gathered into gold. Lit gem-stones stood
on every surface, and on the spancelled air
were five diamond wounds among the wood
whose world was angels, weight was love
from where time was not once but always.

No casual punishment; no criminal news:
everything looked, and all became the night –
fictive, changeable, filled with tomorrow
and the strong stars and hope's thin fingernail moon.
But only I . . . And I was dark, whose mind's not right
among sorry and worry's witness, and only I . . .
I saw more strangeness, saw streamers of light,
pure energy gathered to its oldest source
and worth the world fuse with the living wood;
and through all this, the first, last
original wrong that wrecked the human compass.
Then the right half of the cross began to bleed.

All I could think was worst whose worst was done,
and couldn't be unwished. And look, I was afraid,
but vision wouldn't vanish. Sometimes what stemmed there
was blood, sometimes a stricken beauty
soiled with sweat, or sweet with altered night.

I watched down minutes, decades, trapped in time
whose time was only I and all I might have done,
until I heard a voice behind the air,
another witness; words:

You won't have heard of me, so long ago
I was yet from long ago memory lasts.
Axes at the forest's edge cut me,
men stripped me, stirred me from roots there.
Strong enemies took me, wrought me
to a laughing-stock, a spectacle.
Nothing particular.
Made me (mind) made me carry,
heave up their criminals there,
carried me, fastened me flesh,
set me on the black hill

Golgotha, Golgotha
the hill's harm, hardest
who has a cross to bear
and only I weighed with the wicked
was wicked, worst of all

I watched the kindness of mankind
hurry to hold me, care to catch and climb,
and worst of all not to dare
bend, bow, break was bitter,
though I saw the whole earth's mass move,
could have killed in turn but kept,
stood motionless; might have had might;
did not fell or fall; but failed.

Girded the young one, God Almighty,
strong, stripped on Golgotha,
hauled onto the high gallows,
place of scorn, scourge and the poor skull;
mighty, though, his mood was mighty
and as a man he would release mankind.
And as a man he would release mankind.

I shook, his shoulders on me, shook
and not to dare bend, bow, break
was bitterest, fail to fall;
but had to hold and hold and hurt,
stood fast in age, agony

*Voices:*

    . . . anger and misery
    . . . strangers were everywhere
    . . . you won't have heard of me

*Death*

*But I, who am I, I was raised up,*
*end-long, called rood, called cross,*

*Death*

*king's crucifix, killer*
*whose name is mass and always carries weight*

*Death*

*they drove through me, blood-dark nails;*
*malice they made me, murder made me;*
*and not to bow, break them, not to harm*
*any, not one – can you hear me?*

*Death*

*And harming not one who hurt, hurt Him.*
*Lord, have mercy.*

*Smeared us, mocked, they mocked us both together.*
*I was all, all soiled with blood's stem,*
*was a streaming stem of blood, spoiled*
*from His side after His spirit sent out*
*and died as man before his body died.*

*On the black hill, Golgotha, I will spell out*
*this set down spell out this:*
*I was I, named rood, cross, wrath.*
*I saw, stretched out, racked, ruined,*
*Man who died, who was forsaken then*

*Into Thy hands*

*Dismissal. Stone. Wood. Not one left*
*who wouldn't weep, until the dark*
*covered what was left with cloud*
*as evening shook in shadow. And then*
*whatever also wept*
*whatever made there wept*
*whatever was made there wept,*
*cost a kingdom, king's death, crucifix:*
*Christ died on me, called cross to bear.*
*You didn't think of me, who cried crucify,*
*always anonymous*

*Voices*:

 . . . think of me
 . . . heard of me
 . . . crucify
 . . . forsaken me

Lord, have mercy.

*They came from a little way, a small way off, came to the one I watched as I watched them, worst, wrecked. And I was sorrow, fused with sorrow, bent to their hands, humble. And there they took Him, Almighty God, lifted Him from where He hung, heavy, punished. And they took Him, left me there, left me there to stand driven through by death, wet with blood, wounded, cold. And they laid Him down; the limb-weary they laid down, and stood at His head, torn head, and looked at Him, Lord; and He was rest, eyes closed, tired of struggle, of sorrow, most of me, the gallows-tree.*

(*Voices* continue to share the text)

*They made him a grave, in the sight of His slayer*

*I, Lord, I*

*In the sight of His slayer they carved a bright stone,*
*around the bright stone, morning and night*

*I, Lord, I*

*whose sorrow was song; the song was stone;*
*stone was nightfall and no more to say . . .*

*They came from a little way, always anonymous,*
*saw what they had come to see, and went*

*All but I, Lord, I*

*– and all the crosses, one, two, three,*
*nightfall and the gallows-tree –*

*And went. The corpse cooled, skin stiffened,*
*fair forge of flesh*

*but not I, Lord, I*

*was cut down*
*always anonymous*
*buried*
*anonymous*

*. . . think of me*
*. . . heard of me*

*Time passed, morning and night, men*
*had heard of me, recovered me, here*

*am I, Lord, I*

*as in the beginning*
*am I, a trinity*
*of branches torn from time*
*on the spancelled air lit gem-stones stood*
*at every surface, gold and silver . . .*

*as it was in the beginning.*

*Listener, stranger, this is the telling:*
*sorrow and stone, the worst of wrong,*
*must suffer to witness. And yet*
*whatever was there, not only I,*
*whatever was made there, not only I*
*but men who move, mass on earth*
*and know they are renewed, shall honour me,*
*suffered to witness shall honour me,*

called crucify once. On me God's self
dared in durance, and for that I, also,
haul into heaven, made whole, make whole
any, even one, whose fear I frame.
Once, then, whose dream was all the dark
I had to go, hardest held and hurt,
I learned from death life's way, bought dearest,
the words to tell I am the Word
whose weight is love.

*

CREDO

Credo in unum Deum

Listener, stranger, beloved,
tell this: I am the Way, Truth, Life.
God's self suffered me,
daybreak, nightfall and the gallows-tree,
for the sake of sin, wrong's worst
from Adam's first to last.
Death tasted bitter, Golgotha gall.
And yet from first to last
there was no death. Not only I
but you know mind has mass, not death,
since He rose again, whose mind was mighty
to release mankind, and I believe –
I know and you know

*(Voices 1–3, in chorus)*
I believe in God the Father Almighty,
Maker of heaven and earth,
and in Jesus Christ his only Son our Lord,
Who was conceived by the Holy Ghost,
born of the Virgin Mary, suffered
under Pontius Pilate, was crucified,
dead, and buried. He descended into hell;
the third day He rose again from the dead;
He ascended into heaven, and sitteth
on the right hand of God the Father Almighty.
From thence he shall come to judge

55

*the quick and the dead.*
*I believe in the Holy Ghost;*
*the Holy Catholick Church;*
*the Communion of Saints;*
*the forgiveness of sins;*
*the resurrection of the body;*
*and the life everlasting . . .*

*He will come again to judge,*
*God's self spanning heaven and earth,*
*and judge each one, any, even the least last*
*for what they have earned here*

*an eye's blink between dark and the dark*

*and never to be unafraid, sorry —*

*. . . sorry, you've got no evidence*
*sorry, nothing to recognise*
*sorry, nothing to do with me . . .*

*He will ask, ask any there:*
*this is the Word, whose weight is love;*
*love is these nails, thorns; what hung there, look.*
*This is love, called crucify. Would you be called?*

*And they'll be afraid, and few*
*will know what to begin to say to Christ —*

*sorry, nothing to do with me?*
*sorry, you haven't heard of me?*

*But no one needs sorry. Who suffered to witness*
*I, even I, will help into heaven*

*Amen.*

**John**:

Amen was over, vision, vanished.
I was alone, left stretched out on the tree of life
alone. Who can lift me from the tree of life?
Any, even the least, to love me on the tree of life?

56

Bent to the wood, worst and wrong I prayed –
and hope came, like the thought of travelling
always anonymous, between mind and mind
going the long way, showing what I am
so it is seen what I am not, not lasting,
not durable, but finally in place

*Judas*: *'in isolating me from the objects which surrounded me, in confirming me in my mistrust of the reality of material phenomena, and making me rest in the thought of two and two only supreme and luminously self-evident beings, myself and my Creator'*

*Nauseating self-justification . . .*

*John*:

And my protection is set to this source, called cross to bear.
Friends are gone, the rich once, the powerful once,
all gone to glory, from now on not to greet,
forgetting the world, but no alas or loss
since they live where life is long.
Only I – why left out? – look each day
towards the time I will be first fetched
from the lean world, not lingering,
to where will be the endless, single joined self,
myself, the Word, and all my others breaking bread.

God guide my feet, God who through all earth
dares durance daily on the gallows-tree
He saved us, loved, gave us life to last,
healing us home for blessedness, born again
among the many lost once: not right,
not principled, the first to fail,
but finally by Him healed home,
finally arriving, wrapped in rest.
Amen.

*Miriam*:

I was the crown of thorns, the world of his loss.
I was the nineteen hundred and ninety nine
      nails that drove through the cross.
I was the voice that dragged him home alive
      and then to this.
I was the poison of the poisoned kiss.

You wondered you all wondered why the heart
could be so silent when the wires of hate
      tightened their barbs across
the years of angels. Angels tore me apart,
      were not to trust,
could not explain beyond a bare *You Must*.

I didn't choose.
Whatever's there is always there to lose –
      the weight on a blind cross
hung by the hands on nails that tear . . .
Who faulted him
faults me . . . Someone should close his eyes.

I was the paradise. I was the lies
I was told, the truths I didn't do,
      the meaning of the cross,
I can't bear it. Out of the blue
      immensity
I was the born again, whose face is you.

*

*Elisabeth*:

One went the hammer
      whose echo blow-flies fused on meat.
      Dogs barked at dust; as usual,
      mud fractured in the heat.

Two went the hammer.
      In its kingdom of age houses slept
      the mid-day out; as usual
      no promises were kept.

Three went the hammer.
       Wings scattered somewhere. Out of sight
       a name was cursed, as usual,
       and wouldn't last the night.

Four went the hammer.
       Hands fussed for water, formed on bread.
       Hours tasted wine; as usual,
       very little got said.

Five was the point
       as usual. As usual
              I nailed my Saviour to a tree
                  for company.

★

*He cam also stille*
*ther his moder was*
*as dew in Aprille*
*that falleth on the gras . . .*

**Miriam**:
       Only if I reach out
       to touch him will I feel the weight
       of nails driven through with doubt
       and beauty. But it's come too late –

       Centuries held their breath
       for this: a middle-aged blind girl
       blinded by grief and death
       to death. The flags of nations furl

       into the future, and
       my hand is chaos if it close
       on dew that came to stand
       on crushed petals of the steel rose.

       Dumb. Prayer should be dumb.
       Do what they must. Do what you can.
       I am about to become
       the witch-hunt and the hanging man.

*Mary M*:

She stood just like the others,
looking past the usual wreckage
of hours and stones. A dog did its business
against a shaft of wall. The shops closed
on the anthems of profit and loss.

The sun burned a shadow from a passing cloud.
It was a Friday night, and everyone wondered
if they were on a promise . . .

She stood
as if the nails and wire were good.
Perhaps she didn't know
that all the choices were you,
that all the past came true,
that blood had to flow.

Two thousand years from Now
the silos opened and the boys
applauded for something not gone wrong.
Their shadow applauded too, and in her name
a hundred cities exploded into song
until the sirens, masks and hands
lifted the faces from the wallpaper,
the limbs from their anatomies
of air and dust, and no goodbye.

Perhaps she noticed why
the hours and darkness came
to injury and blame.
She was about to fly.

★

*Miriam*:

Broker the day
to the expensive sky:
the cost of a crucifix.
The dark knows why.

Sit up late
with a damaging glass.
Perhaps it's better . . .
But let it pass.

Sleep if you can.
Make the curtains close.
Shred the blue petals
of the steel rose.

Rub out the date.
Forget the rhyme.
Sell all the anger
and call it time.

Cancel the lamp,
erase the house key.
This death had a meaning.
Its meaning was me.

*Part Two*


VI: HOMILY

*Laudamus te*

**Judas**:

No doubt you are wondering, dear friends, why our esteemed author – and may the ink in his printer never run dry – has chosen one of the most reviled voices in recent history to present this, his latest effusion on a serious subject. To be honest, so am I. I, as you no doubt realise, was fairly, if not absolutely comfortable where I was – the wine was at least drinkable, the women, ostensibly, chaste enough to be a sexual challenge – and to be translated out of an erotic, betraying, post-coital slumber in order to encounter an audience hostile *a priori* to anything one might have to say, is a form of punishment I wasn't anticipating. Death – if it can be called death – seems very unfair sometimes.

'Still,' I hear you mutter, 'didn't you deserve it?'

Before I answer this question – and believe me, it's a question that I want very much to answer – let me say a word about the Other Place. No doubt you have been told, and more than once, that the Other Place is reserved for those who have interfered with a policeman, physically enjoyed that regrettable incident in Berlin, or exultingly clubbed baby seals to death. And further, unreliable sources will have told you that the company There is far from congenial. Not a bit of it – *louche*, perhaps, but in an entertaining if specious sort of way, the sort of way that might, for example, favourably impress an over-anxious visiting mother who wanted to Get to the Bottom of It. In fact, the company is charming, the drugs cheap, the sleep sound if you like that kind of thing, and the girls engagingly pliant, decoratively suitable to be worn for cocktails and sufficiently modest not to create a scene. Frankly, I've quite relished the time I've spent in such admirable and undemanding *ententes*. From your faces, which remind me so much of home, I see we begin to understand each other, despite your – and who would blame you? – initial mistrust. And this makes my small duty today so much more pleasurable, despite its inauspicious origins and the hint of mutual resentment that accompanied my present incarnation. Let's put that behind us. After all, I often do. And at least you will know where I'm coming from, as the Americans rather unfortunately say. It may be true that I am *obliged* to be present – our author (and may the fount of his creativity never dry) has, willy-nilly as one might say, and for reasons best known to himself, deemed me necessary – but perhaps even at this stage we can agree that I am not cast within the parameters of this aural *ensemble* in the ludicrous role of a half-sober Best Man or an implausible dictionary salesman who's just had a non-lexical row with his unglossable wife. At this late stage I have nothing particular to celebrate, no one to give away, and nothing to sell.

'Why then,' I hear you ask, 'is he here?'

In many ways I share your interrogatory puzzle, but before I come back to it – and I will come back to it – let me just answer some of the female frowns I garnered a moment ago. I see from the faces that own them that they belong to the Sisters. 'How dare he' (your outrage says) 'demean the Sisterhood to a cocktail accompaniment? Our splendid potentials to that vile male construct, modesty? Our minds to a Martini umbrella? Our bedroom yelps to chastity?' Of course, dear ladies, you will realise that I was merely employing a figure of speech – and what a figure. Like you, I delight in all manifestations of the sexual muse, and like you, long ago I realised that if the destiny of the opposite sex is to destroy its ontological twin then this had better be done without tears, without recrimination, and without hectoring, overlong, left-wing speeches delivered through an oratory timbre that sulks through Birmingham vowels whose oral gravities are heavy with the bad breath of the implacable. (Not, I hasten to add, that I have anything against Birmingham. Indeed not. The locale inevitably recalls the place from which I have had the hot *frisson* of temporary departure, and I'm sure, dear ladies, that you are mature enough – I see from your faces that you are – to realise that travel, whether it's outward or return, one way or round trip, not only Broadens the Mind but inevitably brings with it the allure of intimate adventure.) In short – and why not? – I'm perfectly willing to concede that in a brittle political sense you are no doubt right to be fractious about what you see as the phallocentricity of my figures of speech. But we are all old enough, I hope, not to confuse rhetoric with reality, and if I speak, if only for a moment, from my own reality, discarding the doubtful props of the homiletic persuader, then the truth – what I might call the naked truth – is that in Birmingham, as in the place I have customarily come to inhabit, as in unstable boudoirs decorated with French blinds, ill-fitting appliances, greasy mirrors, and that rattan cane chair from IKEA (£44.95), the sexual act between consenting partners of whatever gender is *au fond* about power, destruction, and hard cash. As I'm sure you've found, hope does triumph over experience, but then it has to reach for the cheque-book. (In point of fact, Birmingham has profited rather handsomely from such transactions, as the small ads. in a gentlemen's recreational magazine of my acquaintance suggest.) In the Other Place, of course, we have long been obliged to accept that inter-course is a transitive activity for the benefit of interpersonal need, and many of us do well out of the relevant accounts. Everyone seems to be happy with this arrangement: the apparently chaste are well paid, the modest are in demand for the next photo-shoot, and even the most dubi-ous face can be offered a small contract in a forthcoming issue of *The Max: Leg Models Directory*. Ask yourselves, if you will, whether you are in a position, dear ladies, to question the positive choices your co-sexed doubles appear to embrace – particularly when many of your good selves used exactly that meretricious freedom-of-choice argument to justify your own erotic becoming, your abortions, your single parenthoods, and to answer the body in unfortunate sandals who was your most recent inquisitor at GLAA, the gay and lesbian adoption agency. Yes, surely . . . We are – as it were and to all appearances – free to choose, and in my own way I have tried to ensure that the perks of choosing are com-parable to those offered in any other line of gainful employment: the edi-tors I use are on undeclarable expenses, the camera men on generous commission, and genito-urinary inspections are regularly held in a sooth-ing ambient atmosphere (we find Schubert particularly useful in this con-text). And so, if I understand your concerns I have also tried, over many years, to put those concerns into a co-operative framework that brings the benefits of a structured economy to the whole messy, ejaculatory business. I dare say, if I may be allowed to speak for myself and my part-ners and co-proprietors, that across many generations we have done more for the comfort of human need than have the wishes and petitions, the supplications and the ambiguous candles, of the metaphysically pious – those whom I believe you would now call politically correct. Their intentions, like yours, do them credit, but in the circles in which I move it's an article of faith that a credit that doesn't know its own PIN num-ber is a nugatory nonsense, a chimerical mal-adaptation to the wilderness of human desires; which is why, after all, I chose to begin the work of *The Judas Foundation* with thirty pieces of silver – equivalent, strange to say, to the price of a bottle of duty-free designer perfume in today's money. But I anticipate. Enough at present to point out, definitively, that my deep concern for the alternatively gendered finds its inevitable neurological echo in the male psychology of the Anima, that uncom-fortable and often unacknowledged cry of the internally feminine, the She-principle, which has ensured not only the presence of my co-witnesses here but also the survival of Mariolatry through the past two millennia. Perhaps, as you suspect, my recently deployed figures of rhetoric are ill-chosen from your current perspective, but the reality, the truth (if you will) is that I honour the feminine in you – despite your subtly fractious dubieties – because I have no choice but to recognise it in myself. However, again I anticipate, and since I sense your impatience with my digression from what, as you see it, is strictly historical fact, then perhaps you will be good enough to let me say a few words on that significant topic.

'His words,' you say, 'don't square with the books.'

And here I feel on more certain ground, being as I am among a largely literate and cultured *congeries* who import into their reading habits a well-bred dialectic, a distrust of authorial intention (with which distrust, I'm bound to say, our own author is happy to collude), an ill-concealed impatience with footnotes and scholarly apparatus, and a desire to strangle the deliberate pedlar in obscurantism, the young show-off, and the heavy-browed propagandist who has permanently misplaced her sense of humour. Yes, for all our cultural and, if I may put it this way, personal differences, I can tell that we share the same professional skills, and are willing to undergo the usual ritual self-effacements when confronted with that document in permanent dialogue with its own ache of becoming-and-understanding, the Text. And Texts, as we all know from the *nostra* of this post-Structuralist, post-New-Historicist, post-post-Marxist, post-Apocalypticist age, never mean what they appear to say, however loudly they insist on their own terms. Literature, in sum, is not 'about' Life. No, professors and partners, collaborators and complicitors: Literatures – or would you prefer it if I use the more amenable and no-less-accurately descriptive term, *textualities*? – textualities are not, really not, about explaining the present to itself through the imaginary past. Surely we are grown up enough not to make that *jejune* assumption? They – the textualities, the *scriptibles* and *lisibles* of which I speak – are not concerned with human follies, joys, possessions, consciences, histories, defeated loves, futures, or anything at all to do with the necessary illusions of Real Life. No. They are about themselves and each other, more or less in that order. Text talks to text across the conceptual ocean of worry, money, time and desire. The *Beowulf* poet spends a fortune calling the anonymities of *Gawain* to complain that he can no longer alliterate; Jack Donne – a good friend, if I may invoke his persona without compromising his (largely tacit) textual principles – Jack is not, at this moment within which we speak, wiping himself after a delightfully unsatisfactory *rendezvous* with a sullen black whore, but worrying his tapers sick about the apparent fact that his sonnets are full of Gaps; Bill Wordsworth – dear Bill, and such a promising sister – Bill spends hours on the horn to bored John Milton trying vainly to persuade him that he should be living at this hour, while learning constraints on metrical cadences from blindly-dictated replies; and so on. But – and this is my point – these conversations, these anxieties of influence, are just as important for what they don't say as for what they seem to say. Silence, or the misplaced stammer, the gulp of indignation, the rhythmical and syntactic hiatus, the ingressive airstream of literary astonishment – these . . . *Signify*, to use the term correctly via proper Saussurean connotative mechanics. *Logos* is lacuna, and, dear friends and colleagues, we (if I may presume upon plurality) have become increasingly aware that it is up to us to fill in the Gaps. Certainly, this is a heavy responsibility, but it is also a great challenge, and one that I know we can meet with suitable ingenuity – a capacity which, I like to think, we have never entirely lacked. The task, then, as I see it – I'm happy to be corrected, and will take questions later, as I'm sure you've been informed – the task is to teach the Text what it wanted to say if it had only had the courage to say so in the first place, together with its own original wit, a decent dictionary, and a wardrobe of spectacular logorrhoea recently replenished in Paris, Harvard, Stanford and Yale. Looking at you from within this undeserved spotlight, and knowing of your reputations, I feel very confident that we are academically braced for the conceptual rigours, the theoretical innovations, that wait for us along the forward projections of the diachronic axis – which is why I am equally confident that you will join me in bringing a well-reasoned scepticism into the received textualities that seem to have made up the historically-persistent persona that now addresses you, by which, of course, I mean Me.

'Well,' I can hear you thinking, 'what about You?'

I thank you, and sincerely, for asking this question, and in such a pronominally-neutral and uncommitted way. Far be it from me to confuse my synchronic corporeal existence with the psychological and textual pressures you have come to know as 'Judas Iscariot'. It follows from the principles I have just delineated that we are none of us, not even I, about to fall into that phenomenological error. Indeed not. Rather, I am for this purpose, and perhaps *in toto*, better conceived of chiefly as a textual problem, for it is in the inspection of this problem that 'Judas' lies. Consider, if you will, the aberrant and contradictory testimonies of the Four Witnesses. Consider the logical contradictions in the presentation of ostensibly factual material. Consider the Textual Gaps – and having considered them, come to your renewed and renewable opinions as if they were formed by the allure of dispassionate literary conquest: *vraiment sont les plaisirs du texte les plaisirs du monde* – a fact of which, *entre nous*, the Fourth Witness was only too well apprised. And if I begin my analysis with him, this is simply because for all his faults – mystics are tiresomely bibulous at the best of times – he did put his aged finger on one truth that is often overlooked in the biblical hubbub. I quote, then, from the Fourth Witness:

> *Then took Mary a pound of ointment of spikenard, very costly, and anointed the feet of Jesus, and wiped his feet with her hair; and the house was filled with the odour of the ointment. Then saith one of the disciples, Judas Iscariot, Simon's son, who should betray him, 'Why was not this ointment sold for three hundred denarii, and given to the poor?' This he said, not that he cared for the poor, but because he was a thief, and had the bag, and bore what was in it . . .' (John 12: 3-6)*

Let's ignore, for the moment and for the purposes of exposition, the deterministic 'who should betray him' clause, which I read as an unfortunate piece of sly patristic teleology – the Witness was always fond of this parenthetical tactic, largely in order to cover the technical deficiencies in his own oracular style . . . Let us ignore it, together with the unsupported and entirely uncorroborated 'he was a thief' (which I'll address in a moment), and instead let's examine the core of truth embedded in the pith of the testimony. And the truth, friends, is that in these circumstances of highly suspect intimacy I *did* complain about the cost of the actions involved. Nor was I, as I believe the synoptic so-called gospels agree, the only one among the brethren to do so. Simon and Matthias were certainly giving each other intriguingly odd looks. Again, however, I had more reason to query the financial propriety of this kind of melodrama: as John succinctly puts it, although his taste in assonance is questionable, I 'had the bag', that is, one of my many functions was that of Treasurer to the Twelve. Nor should this surprise you, my current auditors, given what the worthy denizens of the Other Place have often referred to as the philanthropic dynamism of *The Judas Foundation*, to which I briefly alluded a little earlier. And if, I say if, I am to be charged with philanthropy, then I'm afraid I must plead guilty. Three hundred denarii – thirty pieces of silver – would have done much, and done so immediately, to relieve the sufferings of the Essenes; they would have allowed the Pharisees to create their own archive library, for the good of future generations of scholars; they would have permitted the Bethany Women's Group – at that time seen with a certain amount of suspicion by the authorities – to form a crèche, staffed by the Young Homeless; and they would have allowed the Samaritans to offer an upgraded service, including their ambitious Soup Kitchen for Amputees, the victims of the latest Pontian (by which naturally I mean Roman) ethnic cleansing. These projects were very much in my mind as I raised towards the pedal nard what was merely a semi-critical eyebrow, which was over-interpreted, in what I suppose was a highly-charged atmosphere, as a point of order. And John, whom I have to say I loved and love as a brother, proved to be the arch over-interpreter. In this, I have to say with regret, he again revealed what the Twelve used to refer to as 'John's Little Problem'. It was, as I believe you will have seen for yourselves from his attitude here today, a problem that came from the bottom of the once and future wine-flask. Small wonder, then, that he and I used to have a few quiet words about his consumption. He never realised, particularly after he'd become the star of his own drinking biography on Patmos, that my intentions were wholly for his own good. 'He was a thief' . . . Dear me, no. I was merely acting with transparent, and even honourable, charity in withholding the next, and the next, chiming *tranche* of John's drinking money. And like many of the vinously-challenged, he had the weakness to become aggressive, abusive, and inaccurate when thwarted of the necessary tincture. Of course it's also true that we all used to turn an incurable blind eye to the problem: myths make their own importance, and John was, even then, prolifically inventive. We thought, wrongly as it turned out, that when the work of the Twelve came to be assessed by the government inspectors that John would prove to be one of our strongest assets, biblio-metrically speaking. But my responsibilities increasingly came to trouble my love. There was so much practical that the Twelve could do with the denarii that John habitually, even, dare I say it, embarrassingly used to massage his throat. And given this, the breathlessly-delineated background, I trust, colleagues, that you can imagine how many of us felt about the apparently trivial matter of the ointment. It was symptomatic of a deeper disorder. Money, as I have shown, I hope, in the Other Place, can and indeed should be put to use. Its only point is philanthropic *haecceity*. It is the structural engineering of every revolution. It is freedom. It makes people happy. And if, as I may I think justly claim, if I was in some ways the first Christian entrepreneur, the whole cultural enterprise was based on the redistribution of wealth – a tenet and a practice which our Leader had explicitly encouraged. In fine, I acted with a certain amount of heart-breaking consistency, and my actions were entirely in accord with the rabbinical principles our Leader had so tellingly enacted in his many speeches and *soi disant* miracles. In return, I am accused of theft. Since this overlooks not only the motives of my historical present but also the actions of my historical future, once more I must remind you of the received biblical veracities, and quote from the First Witness:

*Then one of the twelve, called Judas Iscariot, went unto the chief priests, and said unto them, 'What will ye give me, and I will deliver him unto you?' And they bargained with him for thirty pieces of silver . . .*

*(Matthew 26: 14-16)*

*. . . Then Judas, when he saw that he was condemned, repented, and brought again the thirty pieces of silver to the chief priests and elders, saying, 'I have sinned in that I have betrayed innocent blood.' And they said, 'What is that to us? See thou to that.' And he cast down the pieces of silver in the temple, and departed, and went and hanged himself . . .*

*(Matthew 27: 3-5)*

Notice the textual crux formed by the word *bargained*. The King James Bible, on which many of you cut your Sunday school teeth, has 'covenanted', that is, they promised, rather than bargained. I won't bore you with the original Greek, but make this point only to emphasise how confusing these apparent testimonies can be. However, what none of the gospellers deem worthy of mention is that the infamous – I believe they are infamous – thirty pieces of silver were equivalent, allowing for market fluctuations, to the price of the bottle of perfume that had started all the trouble in the first place. I wanted merely a scant justice, no more, no less. And you will I think agree that it would have been consistent for me, Judas Iscariot, to put that sum to use for the philanthropic purposes that have always been so close to my heart. This is, naturally, why I returned the gift to the authorities after the regrettable incidents on Golgotha. Since I was simply trying to uphold the Law – and had explicitly been urged to do so by our Leader – I thought that it would surely be possible for the relevant authorities to make a better *structural* use of the funds than could my good self, particularly under the circumstances, where all of the Twelve were, in that febrile atmosphere of eschatological confusion, viewed with a covert if not overt mistrust by the general public, depending, of course, on the strength of their admissible sympathies and the received wisdom they were gullible enough to believe would purchase their freedom.

'But if,' I can imagine you asking, 'if you were conscious of no wrongdoing, why did you repent?'

Let me be quite frank. Like the rest of the Twelve, trained in Jewish traditions of the Last Things, the Messianic deliverance, the genealogy of the Branch of David, I had fully believed our Leader when – eventually, and after a great deal of planning – he revealed himself to be the Messiah for which we had waited . . . even if, subsequently, he was not the One for which we had hoped. Like Matthew, like John, like the others, I took the miracles at face value, and in truth I – we all – felt a certain energetic empowerment as we lived through our situation. His calling came with a certain glamour attached to it – the talk-shows, the girls, the dinner invitations, the power breakfasts, the action. But – and I ask you to follow me closely here – after I had made my submission to the authorities I discovered, from unimpeachable sources, that our Leader, far from being the noumenal miracle-worker in whom we fondly and blindly believed, was actually engaged in a goal-directed and even, if you will, secular campaign to subvert the Law, to promote himself as the Messiah despite precedent and his credentials (which were, I think you'll agree, minimal at best), and to destabilise the massive conceptual solidities of the Pharisaic traditions. In short, he was a man, no more. A dreamer. A schemer. Far from suffering through his own inevitable fate, scorned, scourged, derided, acquainted with grief and so forth, he had actually chosen it, and chosen it as a man. I'll go further: he'd not only chosen it, he'd planned it, as the authorities made clear to me over what I increasingly came to see as, in one sense, a squalid transaction. This revelation, as you can I trust well believe, came as something of a shock. And it was in that shocked state that I returned the sum of money that had been covenanted to me for my pains. He suffered as a man – a strategic genius, maybe, but also a deluded innocent who thought he could work the future by writing, and then starring in, his own biography. He had become his own ministry – the Ministry of Propaganda. He had made his own news. No wonder, then, that I felt disappointed and concerned – a concern compounded by the fact that we had all expected a victorious deliverance, the glitter of overthrow, the credit-worthiness that would allow us to develop our post-Messianic charitable projects. We expected a profit. We got instead a donkey, a bad meal, and the verbal and physical abuse of people who should, really, have known better. There might have been rather more in it for us, don't you think? And so, yes, I returned the gift. Yes, I 'repented', under the conditions I've just described. But it's a supreme irony, and one that over the years has caused me some amusement, that to go down in history as the Great Betrayer is the converse of that synchronic reality in and by means of which our Leader had, to all intents and purposes, betrayed us. Although I can smile about it now, it pains me to repeat to you that I acted out of disappointment, not malice.

 'Well, then,' you say, 'why did you hang yourself?'

I'm glad you raised this point, and I welcome the opportunity to clear the matter up. You'll recall, I'm sure, that earlier I enjoined you to look on me as a textual problem, a problem of style rather than that of the offensive and time-intensified odour of self-harm. Nowhere is that dispassion more necessary than in considering this particular literary hiatus. If, for example, you can regard me as a textual problem – and now that you are beginning to know my intellectual style you will, I think, have small difficulty in accepting the general premise – then it is a mere step, a chronological footprint, to considering the charge of self-destruction as an error in transmission. Once more I take the liberty of directing you to two passages from the relevant Witnesses:

*Men and brethren, this scripture must needs have been fulfilled, which the Holy Spirit, by the mouth of David, spoke before concerning Judas, who was guide to them that took Jesus. For he was numbered with us, and had obtained part in this ministry. Now this man purchased a field with the reward of iniquity; and falling headlong, he burst asunder in the midst, and all his bowels gushed out. And it was known unto all the dwellers at Jerusalem, insomuch as that field is called in their proper tongue, Akeldama, that is to say, The field of blood.* (Acts 1: 16-19)

*And the chief priests took the silver pieces, and said, It is not lawful to put them into the treasury, because it is the price of blood. And they took counsel, and bought with them the potter's field, to bury strangers in. Wherefore, that field was called, The field of blood, unto this day.*
(Matthew 27: 6-9)

'And all his bowels gushed out.' Peter always did have a gift for the vulgarly melodramatic. Naturally, it served the purpose of the Twelve to broadcast that Judas had come to A Bad End. Every failed revolution needs its sacrificial victim. *Judas in Tree Terror* trumpeted *The Jerusalem Post. Judas Wept* punned *The Bethany Bugle. Iscariots of Fire* gloated *The Jericho Journal* unconvincingly. *Stock Market Crash* reported *The Pilate* – whose leader writer was clearly acting under orders, or the influence, or both. Once Peter and James had put the media machine into action, its taste for the awful headline was rivalled only by its regrettable penchant for designer leisure-wear: a lurid and pointless exercise in damage-limitation. No, colleagues. The truth – which is, as my dear friend Oscar once remarked, seldom pure and never simple – the truth is that I had urged my erstwhile Pharisaic co-transactors, *sotto voce* of course, to see what they could do with my free cash gift and the potter's field. On my way to Bethany that unfortunate Friday (being, as you can imagine, *persona non grata* with certain faces with a penchant for violent ignorance), I had happened to pause for a moment with a friend from the Surveyor's

71

Department of the Ministry of Reconstruction, and had climbed the much-mentioned tree merely to provide an angle for his theodolyte, or whatever impedimenta it is that Roman engineers are in the habit of breaking and charging to the company. I had thought that perhaps the field might serve very well as a site for a Donkey Sanctuary, of which, as you will no doubt be able to imagine, the Promised Land had a veritable dearth. Lazarus, I recall, was particularly hard on his beasts . . . But at the *moment juste*, as the angles had been corrected and the cornerstones were forming incipiently from sun-baked mud in my Roman friend's calcu-lable eye, a peal of thunder, altogether unexpected, startled a starling's nest, which startled me into a tragic and wasteful loss of balance, with the results you can guess. *Akeldama* . . . Forgive my mirthless rictus of laugh-ter. You thought it was my blood? The blood of strangers? Not a bit of it. They used the field forever afterwards as a donkey burial ground, and limed it at weekends – Saturdays, naturally, excepted. It was just a pity that the Sanctuary never, if I can put it this way, got off the ground. I'm sure you appreciate the ironies involved. But of the final irony you may need notice, since it seems to have gone unremarked in the dark forward and abysm of time, and the irony is this: if our Leader, 'Son of God' and 'Son of Man' – titles, I ought to add, which he habitually used for the simple purposes of anonymity – if our Leader had foreknowledge, as God, of the events on Calvary, then naturally he would have had fore-knowledge of the role I was to play in his unnecessary tribulations. This must be at least a reasonable assumption. And I say to you: *of course he did*. He was a brilliant temporal manipulator, a metaphysical wizard, a poli-tically speculative, ambitious, even worldly man. You have only to think for a moment of his reply to my innocent question 'Is it I?' His reply? 'You have said' – and the ghost of a wink crossed his eye. I was, in the final analysis, part of his intention, a function of his will. I was meant to act as I did. And so, dear friends, you are meant to act as you do. 'The lot of man is chosen,' as someone – Willie, I think – once remarked.

    'Ah,' you rejoin, with a sussurating ripple of dissatisfaction, 'but where does that leave free will?'

To which I say, if you will forgive me lapsing into a dialect I have come to find intimately pleasing, *will-schmill*. Knox and Calvin – who have since become very good friends, and I'm sure you remember them from sixth-form History, together with the Diet of Worms – the Johnnies (as I call them) were really quite correct. You and I are all written down in the book of fate. *There is no such thing as free will.* Our actions are as pre-determined as our genetic make-up – our dextrousness, our nervous tic that resembles our grandmother's, our bad tempers (so like father), and our penchants and aptitudes for music or chess or an easy lay. *We cannot choose.* We only think we can, and it is by that illusion that men are pleased to live. Illusion on illusion: 'mirror on mirror, mirrored is all the show,' or, more strongly I suppose, 'from nowhere into nowhere nothing runs.' A fine poet, Willie, even if he doesn't like games and is not the joiner-in I would have hoped. But he had it almost right: we live with the illusions of choice, the mirror of Self, the Acting, Choosing Self. (*Laughs.*) The self? The . . . Self? Sterile nonsense. Few people in this room, let us suppose, have any real notion of what Self they mean by Self, of the ramifications of their endless, recontextualisable, and linguistically-defined, plurality or the irradiations of their genetic, co-historical, and usually regrettable inheritances. Would that we did: it might avoid much heart-ache. For – perhaps you'll allow me to put it this way – *if everything is pre-determined, then everything is permitted.* There are no right choices, since right choosing will come to the same end as wrong. There are no more decisions to take, no risks to run, no face to please or praise, gain or negate. There is no garden of forking paths; there is only a bare, level plain where the horizon is never visible however far you travel, and where the only possibility of continued existence is what Nietzsche – and may we, simply for the temporary purposes of argument, bless his name – called the Joyful Wisdom, the wisdom of acceptance. We simply are: suffering is an illusion, it has already been chosen; love is an illusion, its next date has already been written into the calendar of endeavours; even death – the big event, the Marian intercession, the priests and doctors doing their unsteady best to help the corporeal into the unreality of extinction – even death . . . I can do no better than remind you that 'Man has created death' in the spectacular distortions of the hall of mirrors, just as he has created the hall of mirrors from a hand-ful of desert dust. And the biggest death, the grandest illusion, the end-less *trompe l'oeuil*, is what hung and is hanging, wailing as usual, from a tree at an unspecified point in time in a dirty city on a minor trade-route. I'm very tempted to think that he will never die, but perhaps he's just appalled by the view. Perhaps, after all, the incident was not merely what he deserved, but what he expected, intended, planned, and delivered. It's really quite heart-breaking, if you think about it along the lines I'm sug-gesting. But ultimately, if we have no free will, no choice, and no hope, then the gestural sacrifice is of no more moment to human history than a broken clock or a completed crossword. They have fulfilled their func-tion. They are no longer anything to do with us. They hold no theory of time, no conjectural lexicon for the faint of heart. We are merely obeying impulses we don't understand in order to develop the illusions of our Selves for a purpose that has already been fixed, did we but know it – which we don't. We are, in short, only acting under orders – except that no one can reconstrue what the orders were, and someone has thrown away the hard copy and write-protected the relevant disk. Hope? No. Change? No. Love? Only a little defeated tenderness (which, in its way, has a certain erotic charm). Let us not fool ourselves. We are too grown up, and some of us are too old, for that.

And so, my dear friends, I am instructed by our author (and may his pen never finally glean his teeming brain) that it's time to come to a suitably illusory close. Since I have taken rather longer than I expected to analyse the truths we have come to inhabit – and I thank you and our author for this unexpected liberty – perhaps you will allow me, if only briefly, to summarise the main points I have tried, however clumsily, to make.

First, you won't need me to remind you not to believe all you read. Real Life is a fiction commented on by otherwise-unemployable logorrhoeics who have temporarily, or even permanently, mislaid their neural equipment. Many of them, I regret to say, are American, but at least one is of German extraction. Textuality, on the other hand, is ours, and now. *Carpe diem.*

Second, do not believe all you hear. The aural hustings are a ludic joust which may provide minimal entertainment after a good dinner, but that is all. The serpent and Eve were eventually reconciled, so why waste time?

Third, obey the letter of the law, even if you show contempt for its spirit. I say to you that it is better for an honest man to act on every desire providing he completes his income tax self-assessment form and returns his library books.

Fourth, redistribute wealth, and you will find it returning to you, usually with interest attached.

Fifth, interpret history creatively, and with a knowing smile. No one will ever guess you are as baffled as they look, and you will gain useful credit into the bargain – as I myself have found.

Sixth, be tolerant, conceptually generous. The horizon is still not in sight, nor will it ever be, and we have a long way to travel. The meaning is in the waiting, maybe, but the waiting may as well be good-tempered. Deals can always be done, accommodations can always be reached. Intrigue is invariably more entertaining than principle, and you might like to try it.

And seventh, remember those watchwords Faith, Hope, and Charity. 'Faith is that by which men live' – and includes No-Faith, as I trust I've explained, although your very culture prevents me from putting matters as succinctly as I usually manage in my messages to Death

Row. Hope (ah! hope) includes – it even seduces, for the delight of exquisite pain – No-Hope, and we had better get used to it. Charity is the quality you have extended to me here today, and let me say once again how very grateful I am for your patience, your interventions, and your trust.

Regrettably, dear friends, we have no time for questions as I had hoped, but for those hard of hearing, understanding, eyesight, or any combination of the three, you'll find these seven points treated more generally, and in large print accompanied by humorous political cartoons, in my new book, *Just Judas* (The Serpent Press, £9.95pb/$16.58 inc. sales tax) in which you might like to browse. Signed copies are available at the back of the room. All major currencies are acceptable, and credit cards are, of course, welcomed.

Thank you. And, good people, Ahy-men.

*Part Three*

VII: Agnus Dei

*Domine Deus, Agnus Dei*

*Voice #1*:

**Psalm 23**: The Gathering

I call Him Shepherd, since I am the heard,
lacking in everything except the Word,
Who promised I would lie
all latter spring in birdsong and the sky,
that I would wait beside the sun-struck marl
of rivers harvesting, cool watergrain.

This makes, undoes and remakes what I am: a fall
of brightness like a dale-head stream, the long affinities
of water, home, and chance; and choice to please.

Even if I walk through the valley of
the shadow of death, I want to name it love,
for what has made me want is with me, and
I know the gathering purpose of its hand,
the climate of perpetual afternoon
where clouds cast moving shadows on the land.

To turn for home, and find
after the vanishing journey the table spread;
to sit and eat with guests
and comfortable strangers who renew the ease
of meeting over wine and oil;
to see the past come true, and come to good:

He makes me realise
that though I walk through mercy, still my eyes
are sacrifice, though looking can never end
the grace of place and peace this may intend.

He fed me from cold ground, from ache's mistake
and joy. The final gate is open, chosen
to be recognised. The gathering just won't break.

*

*Voice #2*:
>Lamb of God
>>who taketh away the sins of the world

>You know and I know
>>(always anonymous)
>no mind has mass, but

>I am that I am

>only the noise of the sand
>the desert and the wind on the sand
>in the dry alfalfa
>in the shade of the chameleon
>the picked-clean, sun-struck skull
>of the lamb
>and the taste of the thorn
>and the scorpion –

>No mind has mass

>No?

>Know?

>(*Voices in chorus*): No.

>In this world virgins are raped and there are no miracles.

*

*Voice #1*:
>Who taketh away the sins of the world?
>Somehow, anyhow
>it's too late
>to take the world and its weight away,

77

since the world's already gone
into the stones and sun,
the profit of the mass,
the famine and the fire-bomb.

*Voice #2*:

Who taketh away the sins of the world?
Tell it to the marines
who vanished twice
into the rainbow stains
of an oil-scarred sea,
clutching at Rosary,
becoming their remains,
then air, then ice.
They vanished twice.

*Reports of casualties suggest
it was a successful operation,
code-name Scorpion . . .*

No mind has mass,
just sacrifice.

*Voice #3*:

Who taketh away the sins of the world?
We don't want
we don't need
the sins taking away, the seed
of doubt, the outright lie,
the blemished bed,
the knife, the life, the suicide,
the randy vicar and the teenage bride –
there'd be no breadlines,
no headlines,
no news.
We need your sins
so we can tell you your views:

you're History
your Need to Diet
you're unfit
a Better You for '99

Gotcha
Victory
What to Do about Fat
What to Do
about That Love-Handle
Supermodel
in UFO scandal

(*chant*)

Sin, Fat
Sex- Sin- Fat

you're the mass
you're a mess
you're the pro-le-ta-ri-*at*

**Voice #2**:

Man is born free
and is everywhere
a victim
and a photo-opportunity.

(A smile's on the face
of defeated Grace
as she learns too late
to wait and be happy
(her agent says).
Her agent says
she'll be very good
Hollywood.)

**Voice #1**:

Who taketh away the sins of the world?
Tell it to the love on the dole,
the twice-used cigarettes,
the Can't Afford It blues.
Tell it to next-door's cat
and the repossessed Welcome mat.
Tell it to the Capulets,
tell it to the Montagues.

Tell it to the kid
who can play out when the weather's good
but whose friends can't come round –
too much mess, too much fuss.
She carries the loss
all life, like an incubus.

Tell it to the suit who recruits
the Third World debts
in his fat limousine
in his fine overcoat with the fine mohair sheen.

Tell it to the blind man in Bombay
in Piccadilly Gardens
in the Tuileries
in Watts

Try telling him to call the shots
with his sawn-off legs and the empty soul
of his begging-bowl

*Smile, please*

(**Voices #1-3** *share the text*):
Who taketh away the sins of the world?
    No mind
    no matter
    no weight
    or mass enough
to take away the sin
to let the wound begin
to heal the love
that was the force
that raised the cross

*Smile, please*

A smile like a file
on the television news,
on the toothpaste glitz
of very good
Hollywood

Of course
no mind has mass

*Kyrie, Kyrie*

In this world
smile

you are free

to obey

★

*Voices #1-3*:

Out of the Negev            The Land of Moriah
Always anonymous            No proper identity
Sun and chameleon           Fire, stone and scorpion

      Abraham, Abraham

No point in grumbling        He's a hard task master
Hard on the animals          Cruel to the family
They say he's been through it  They say he got over it

      Abraham, Abraham

Why such an early start?      Can't say for certain now
Taking the compasses          On to the mountain-fall
Fire, stone and scorpion      The sun always kindling

      Abraham, Abraham

Some kind of offering         One kind of sacrifice
Nothing particular            We've got no evidence
Anger and misery              Nothing to place us there

      Abraham, Abraham

Travelling northerly          Into the hinterland
Out of identity               No point in grumbling
There were the four of us     Two cursing voices

      and Isaac, and Abraham

★

81

*And Abraham rose up . . .*

It was too late to run or say goodbye.
We'd sweated up the hill, unpacked the wood
and set it down, and made a meal. The sky
was burnt, and we found shade, and called it good
to rest, not knowing what was happening
except they walked away and we ate bread.
Only after a while, the furrowing
of almost-silence with the drift of smoke,
and the animal gone into the gathering
afternoon where all the sunlight broke
inside the prisms of a half-closed eye,
it was too late to run or say goodbye.

Who's to know? We saw them distantly,
the young one carrying the kindling, and
his father striking fire as he went by
the farthest dunes, then out into the sand.
So what? Nothing to do with us, we thought,
and laid a bet how soon the two would send
back word the thing was done, and the fire caught.
What could we do? If on the master's word
we waited, it was secrecy he'd bought,
as usual, the never seen or heard.
But who's to know? And no one can deny
it was too late to run or say goodbye.

Still, no word came, and on the usual sky
an hour made itself. The bet came off,
and we got up and stretched, and went to try
to find the animal, and gather stuff
the sun could fettle to another blaze –
since sacrifice needs washing, to defy
whatever god there is the poison days
of human hand, ruined by dirt and earth,
fingernail's corruption and filth's trace.
And Abraham, an old man at the birth
of something to appease, was piety
itself – too old to run or want goodbye.

We stopped the grumbling and the laughter then,
cresting a ridge of stones, and looking where
the boy had made a pyre that afternoon,
as knife was braided to a flash of air.
But not a lamb. Tied to the wood with ten
tight turns of hemp, the lad was angled there
as if he expected nothing but amen.
But we were late to run or shout goodbye,
the blade cut downward, and the wood and dune
were flame. To find, to force or satisfy
the gods . . .

No human noise, only the heat's core
spitting the instants god had waited for.

| | |
|---|---|
| We were too late to run | Nothing to place us there |
| You've got no evidence | Is this off the record? |

*Unconfirmed reports are just coming in from Moriah that a teenager has been burnt to death in what seems to have been a holiday accident. The teenager, an only child, is alleged to have been on a back-packing trip with his father at the time of the incident. Further details will follow in our ten o'clock bulletin . . .*

★

**Mary M**:
    . . . And Abraham rose up, and slew his son,
    and half the seed of Europe, one by one.

**Judas**:
But friends, dear friends and colleagues, of course you will say

| | |
|---|---|
| 'This is outrageous | This is a travesty |
| Just look at Genesis | This isn't biblical |
| Has no veracity | Perhaps it's a metaphor' |

Abraham? Abraham?

And in truth I can see, naturally, your point of view. But our task, if you remember, is *to tell the Text what it would have said if only it had had the courage, the wit, and the available structures to say so in the first place.* And what we're confronted with here is, simply, a Text, and one shackled, inevitably, to the social conditioning and the cultural sufficiencies of its own making. And if we ask – let us say, if we interrogate – the Text about the conditions of its own becoming, what do we find?

We go in search of miracles, the sources of the primal Text, the ache of becoming, the contextual dialogues whose point is the necessity of *invention*. And what do we find? Precisely: an invented god. An invented sacrifice. That is not to claim, of course, that the 'story' of Abraham, in the rendering you have just heard, is as lacking in (to coin a phrase) parablistic or, perhaps better, prefigurative substance as the European plasticities of the myth of Father Christmas. Not at all.

I will tell you, if you will allow me to do so, why it is possible, even likely, that the story you have just witnessed is, if not 'true' in the usual simplistic sense, then (if you will) imaginatively real.

First, the god invented by Isaiah – or, more accurately, by his cultural *milieu* – is a god of sulks. He is, among other things, an endlessly unsatisfied silence. He suffers, apparently, from a kind of conceptual constipation. Just listen to him:

> *To what purpose is the multitude of your sacrifices unto me? saith the Lord; I am full of the burnt offerings of rams, and the fat of fed beasts, and I delight not in the blood of bullocks, or of lambs, or of he-goats. When ye come to appear before me, who hath required this at your hand to tread my courts? Bring no more vain oblations; incense is an abomination unto me; the new moons and sabbaths, the calling of assemblies, I cannot bear; it is iniquity, even the solemn meeting. Your new moons and your appointed feasts my soul hateth; they are a trouble unto me; I am weary of bearing them. And when ye spread forth your hands, I will hide mine eyes from you; yea, when ye make many prayers, I will not hear. Your hands are full of blood . . .*
>
> (*Isaiah* 1: 11-15)

A charming picture. Still, to such a created entity, sphincters straining at the tight-packed ordure of mythic offal, perhaps a human sacrifice might have proved a satisfactorily impressive novelty, despite the risks attached to the consumption of red meat. (I apologise, and sincerely, if these images disturb the vegetarians and the health-conscious among you.) But more to the point, in this context, is god's apparent, if nauseating, reasonableness, which is evidenced some few verses adjacent to the passage you have just heard:

> *Come now, and let us reason together, saith the Lord: though your sins be as scarlet, they shall be as white as snow; though they be red like crimson, they shall be as wool . . .* (*Isaiah* 1: 18)

And this leads me to my second point. I hope I am not alone in interpreting this significant passage in ways that challenge its *superficies*. Even the puns have not been lost in translation: *scarlet*, for example – which I read, surely correctly, as *scar – let*, that is, a scar (knife-wound, sacrificial mark) which has been 'let', either 'allowed' or 'rent/extended' (think, for example, of your current English phrase *to let out* a garment). And similarly, it hardly seems necessary – in fact it is otiose – to point out the homophone *red* and *read*. 'Though they be read like crimson' . . . The phrase is simultaneously more and less than what it appears to say, and being so, positively invites creative mis-interpretation ('wilfully inevitable misreading', call it what you will). And the Gospel Witnesses, like the redactor of *Isaiah*, did not disappoint, reinterpreting the Ur-Text, the primal scream of sacrifice, as an act of *substitution*, where, mired in bathos, a hapless ram was textually substituted for the unfortunate youth, Isaac.

Yes, Abraham really did kill Isaac on the desert rise (which, with a blinding and obviously intentional irony, was later the *locus* for the temple of Solomon – *mountain*, I need hardly remind you, was originally a Hebrew symbol for 'kingdom, authority, rule'). But the textual transmission of the act clearly invited misprision of the original *logos*, and, you will recall, *logos* is lacuna, and it is up to us to fill in the Gaps. Therefore, in the tension of Isaiah's rewriting, animal is substituted for human, while thematically, the text retains the authority of its original obedience.

No wonder the Gospel Witnesses found the passage charged with metaphoric power. They, like us, are caught by the narrative, by the horns of textual transmission. Isaac, on this re-reading, prefigures Christ: he is a figure obedient even to death; Abraham is recast into the mould of a loving father who wouldn't spare his own son, etc. etc. Must I, really, draw out these tedious symmetries for you? And last, a ram is substituted for the original human sacrifice, just as our Leader was 'offered' instead of the so-called sins of the so-called world.

*And Abraham rose up, and slew his son . . .*

I hope, I trust, that I have said enough to convince you that this sacrifice, in its Ur-form, positively required both nominal substitution, and thematic misreading. Again I say, do not believe all you hear: it has already been inscribed into the book of the art of misprision, and this Text, like (if you will permit me) the Text of Judas Iscariot, many mean something completely different from what it appears to mean, massaged as it is by the pressures of the diachronically unstable word and the cultural (re)conditioning that forces our endless attempts at (re)interpretation.

And speaking of reading, may I take this opportunity of reminding you that my new book, *Just Judas*, is available via the Serpent Press? Cash or credit-card sales are perhaps . . .

> ***John***:
>
> Enough. Enough.
>
> Throw away the calendar,
> the critical key;
> cancel the cleverness
> that calls you free.
>
> Discard the cheque-book,
> the doubtful receipt;
> all of your enterprise
> means your defeat.
>
> Look back at history
> as it pours into space
> and into the mirror
> of your disgrace.
>
> Run to the libraries,
> flock to the play;
> any diversion
> can please today:
>
> the comfort of strangers,
> the dubious sex,
> gorging on glances
> a moment wrecks;
>
> a theory of money,
> the cash paradigm,
> leads to the precipice
> men made of time;
>
> the forks and faces,
> the glabrous paté –
> you choke on the fish-bones
> and sweat Chardonnay.

Stop conversation,
ignore what you hear,
but still time's falling
from the edge of fear.

Resentment and ruin
worry in the speech,
intending conclusions
they can never reach.

Forget the scholarship,
tear up the degree:
the success you paid for
was temporary.

Temporary the culture,
transient the friend,
momentary the lovers
love can't defend.

Efface the manuscript,
send back the drink:
fatuous alcohol,
purposeless ink.

There's only forgetting,
there's memory's spoil.
But into the absence
flow blood and oil.

I call it sacrament,
you call it waste.
But I eat Christ's body
with its bitter taste.

And there in the Eucharist
a seven-horned lamb,
the end of the sacrifice:
I am that I am.

★

I am that I am

only the noise of the sand
the desert and the wind on the sand
in the dry alfalfa
in the shade of the chameleon
the picked-clean, sun-struck skull
of the lamb
and the taste of the thorn
and the scorpion –

In this world
nothing is what it seems

dead ends and chromasomes,
the neural networks, soft stuff of mass

are becoming air
are becoming memory
are becoming dreams

## VIII: BENEDICTUS

*Benedictus qui venit*

**Voice #1:**

> In this world
> > virgins are raped,
> > > and there are no miracles
> > > > *without the pattern of god-likeness in us.*

**Voice #2:**

> In this world
> > the sky is dark,
> > > and there are no resurrections
> > > > *without the pattern of god-likeness in us.*

**Voice #3:**

> In this world
> > you know and I know
> > > no mind has mass
> > > > *without the pattern of god-likeness in us.*

★

**Elisabeth:**

> And there was no god-likeness in us,
> only the observances,
> the neighbours, the Welcome mat,
> the long evenings with the television
> and the nights drawing in,
> the detailed construction
> of what passed for life
> in the lessening allure of life
> and its small conversation.
> We would look at each other
> > from time to time
> > and say
> > > and say
> we would look at each other from time to time,
> out of the dwindled compass

out of the mirror
out of the candleflame
and the Holy Name,
waiting for someone to call,
but there was no god-likeness in us.
And he would get up and go out, go out,
walk about in the middle of the night
trying to pray, expecting the miracle,
waiting for someone to call,
always right, always right.
But there was no god-likeness in us.
We sat together, lug to lug,
like old sacks of corn
propped on the corner
of the expensive sofa.
There was nothing there to be born.
What can be born
from the used-up crossword,
from the failed nerve
that can no longer drive,
from the dislike you reserve
for someone you've hurt
and then kept alive?
What can be born
but the torn-off stub of time,
the transactions of days
recorded in the cheque-book,
the spiteful look, the vanished glaze
going, going, gone?
The days were just a theory of the sun.

*Without the pattern of god-likeness in us*
we are merely
a forsaken star with a suburban address,
we are just
old people whose culture is unfortunate biology
and the immediate
environment, the ironing-board and the toilet,
the meldable stuff
that comprises the flab
of a corpse on a slab,
its blent compulsions testable by

the surgeon's steel, the Bunsen flame,
the meals on wheels, the social worker's profile,
not the Holy Name.

But why did I wait?
There was a name.
His name was John.
And he was great
in the sight of the Lord . . .

**Judas**:

Another parent saying this was Elijah.
Laughable, really.
Not that it mattered.
I am not what I am.

**Elisabeth**:

. . . And he was great
in the sight of the Lord
even as I felt him move
soundlessly, endlessly,
like the weight of ocean
unfathomed pressure
and fracture
whose weight was love
that something should be born
out of the desert
out of the paid-for house
out of age, and the end of age.
I was the same book
with the same look
but another hand had turned the page.

**Miriam**:

And I was glad, I, I
who had been about to fly.
And who knows best how to say about glory?
Glory's forever around.
You and I, you and I didn't look for glory.
But glory was found.

And my heart magnifies the Lord
and my spirit moves with God my Saviour
as he remembered me and remembers me
when I was the crown of thorn,
the lowest estate, the world of his loss,
the generation of his wound;
when I was the nineteen hundred and ninety-nine
nails that drove through the cross
still glory was found,
and remembers me from generation
into generation:
as time must move
its name is love,
and I was blessed.
The would-be good, the appointed great,
the proud, the talkers, the far too loud
he has brought
to their true estimate;
the low, the lonely, the ones on the street,
the man in the dock, the one who screams
as the key turns in the lock,
he has put right.
And I was blessed by dreams.
The empty belly, the hungry hand he has fed,
and avarice and the need of greed,
the averted eye
of the passer-by,
he has bled.
And I was blessed.
As time must move
its weight is love,
and he shall come to the aid
of the exhausted, the famished,
the barely paid, the about to be sacrificed –
and this was promised
to Abraham, Abraham,

and this was born
in Bethlehem, Bethlehem
where glory was found

in time,
whose cry was love
not once but always.

*

*Dona nobis pacem*

**Voices**:

You know and I know
no mind has mass
*without the pattern of god-likeness in us.*

And this is love, called crucify
before it can be called
'you can be called
the resurrection and the life'.

Without the pattern of god-likeness in us,
out of the vagrancy of days and choice,
out of betrayal, out of malice,
after the Word has been heard unheard,
still
      still
you know and I know
no mind has mass.

Who calls it sacrament?
You call it waste.
So who eats Christ's body
with its bitter taste

*without the pattern of god-likeness in us*
*without the pattern of god-likeness*
*without the pattern*

without release?

After the Word has been heard unheard

only
        only
from mercy, goodness
is time's weight and place.
Grant us its peace.